Original title:
Pinecone Poetry

Copyright © 2025 Creative Arts Management OÜ
All rights reserved.

Author: Nathaniel Blackwood
ISBN HARDBACK: 978-1-80567-167-1
ISBN PAPERBACK: 978-1-80567-466-5

Shadows of the Tallest Trees

Underneath their leafy hats,
Squirrels play a game of splats.
Acorns bounce and giggles rise,
While birds perform their wacky cries.

Sunlight peeks through branches wide,
A shadow dance, the woods provide.
Tree trunks blush in shades of green,
Nature's stage, a funny scene.

Where Earth Meets the Sky

Clouds in line, like sheep at play,
Balloons of laughter float away.
The sun pretends to wiggle bright,
As breezes tease, an airy plight.

Grassy hills are laughing too,
Tickling toes with morning dew.
Butterflies in silly flight,
Chase each other, pure delight.

A Delicate Symphony of Seeds

Seeds are dancing, take a chance,
In a lively, sprightly prance.
Wind gives them a twirl and spin,
Like tiny twisters, let's begin!

Sprouts are giggling as they bloom,
In the garden, there's no gloom.
Petals flutter in a jig,
Nature's choir, oh so big!

Portraits of the Silent Grove

Trees stand tall with grinned old faces,
Sharing tales in leafy places.
Roots below, they tickle deep,
While owls giggle, half-asleep.

Mushrooms wear their silly hats,
Making jokes with chittering bats.
In this grove of silent cheer,
Nature's laughter, loud and clear.

The Echoing Pathways

On winding trails, we skip and hop,
Laughter mingling as we plop.
A squirrel scolds us from a tree,
"Stop making noise, it's just me!"

Through leafy whispers, secrets flow,
The bees can't keep from running the show.
As echoes bounce from bark to crest,
Nature giggles, we feel blessed.

Dreaming in Layers

Underneath the vibrant sky,
We build a fortress, oh so high.
With twigs and leaves, our dreams take flight,
A castle made of pure delight.

In slumber deep, the branches sway,
Whispering tales of silly play.
The moon peeks in, a cheeky grin,
"Did you dream of nuts?" starts the din.

Petals and Pines

Among the trees, we dance so free,
Petals twirling, oh so glee.
A pine tree winks, so full of cheer,
"Can I join you?" it asks, sincere.

With needles sharp, it prances around,
Making friends with flowers on the ground.
Together we laugh, and oh, what fun,
In nature's circus, we're never done.

A Tribute to Winter's Calm

In icy realms where snowflakes twirl,
We make snowmen, give them a whirl.
Their carrot noses, crooked and bright,
Wave to the birds, perched in delight.

Hot cocoa spills as we shiver wide,
Three marshmallows topple, oh what a slide!
Winter chuckles, with frosty breath,
"Is this my new way to scare you to death?"

The Circle of Life

In the forest, nuts do roll,
Squirrels dance, they lose control.
Branches sway, a laughter spree,
Nature's joke, come climb a tree.

Sunlight tickles through the leaves,
Every critter wears its sleeves.
Joyful chaos, seeds in flight,
Life's a party, day and night.

In the Heart of Evergreen Silence

Whispers rustle in the glade,
A raccoon in a masquerade.
Bark's a canvas, tales untold,
Knots and grooves, a sight to behold.

Fungi giggle at the roots,
Witty mushrooms in sharp suits.
In this realm of green delight,
Every shadow's full of light.

Pine Dreams

In a forest of green, where the tall trees sway,
The pine needles whisper, 'Let's play all day!'
They plot little capers, like sneaky old elves,
Hiding their laughter deep down on the shelves.

The squirrels are giggling, as they race up and down,
While branches are bobbing, not making a frown.
With a bounce and a leap, oh what fun they seek,
In the movie of nature, there's always a sneak.

The pinecones get ready, for a toss in the air,
But sometimes they tumble, with a comical flair.
They land on the heads, of unsuspecting folks,
Bringing smiles and laughter, like playful old jokes.

So next time you're wandering, beneath those tall pines,
Listen closely for giggles, in the soft sunshine.
For in the grand forest, amid the tall beams,
Lies a world full of laughter, and very sweet dreams.

Daylight Shadows

As daylight stretches, shadows play tag,
With giggling figures, like a friendly rag.
They dance on the pavement, in splashes of fun,
Playfully ducking away from the sun.

The bumblebees buzz, with a whimsical tone,
While shadows do cha-cha, and groove on their own.
Each leap and each hop, bringing smiles all around,
In this comical ballet, pure joy can be found.

The trees do the tango, while clouds have a laugh,
Joking with sunlight, on their playful path.
The warmth of the day, wraps all like a chow,
While shadows keep frolicking, taking a bow.

So if you see them, don't blink or you'll miss,
A shadowy party, filled with bliss.
With a wink and a wave, they invite you to play,
In the world of daylight, where giggles hold sway.

The Wisdom of the Woodlands

In a forest deep where wisdom grows,
The trees tell tales, as the soft wind blows.
Squirrels chatter about acorn schemes,
While owls nod off in their leafy dreams.

Beneath the boughs, the mischief plays,
Chipmunks dance in the dappled rays.
A rabbit jumps, then takes a bow,
For woodland antics, it's time to chow.

The ancient oaks share gnarled jokes,
While mushrooms laugh at the sneaky folks.
Fungi whisper secrets, a moldy sort,
Of forest pranks in the mossy court.

The pine needles fall with a gentle thud,
And the wise old cypress just shakes with mud.
In the heart of the woods, where laughter's the key,
Wisdom's wrapped up in each silly tree.

Stories Rounded in Scales

Along a river, the fish take heed,
Gathering round for a tale or two indeed.
The frogs sing songs with a croaky flair,
While turtles watch with a shell-back stare.

Bubbles rise up with stories untold,
In the scale-slick realm where the myths unfold.
A catfish boasts of a legendary bite,
While minnows giggle in the fading light.

The otter twirls with a splash and a flip,
As the water snakes gossip and wiggle their grip.
A wise old pike gives a thoughtful grin,
As all her fishy friends gather in.

With scales all a-glimmer and tales all a-spin,
The river's alive, let the laughter begin!
Nature's comedy, rolled up in the flow,
In the stories of scales, there's always a show.

Pinecone Letters

In the forest's post office, the letters soar,
Pine needles writing on the forest floor.
With acorn caps sealing important news,
The woodland critters can't help but snooze.

A letter from the fox, oh what a prank!
Said he spotted a hare and admired its flank.
The squirrel sent word, 'I'm hoarding my stash!'
But the raccoon's off for a trash can bash.

Emails from owls with wisdom so light,
Wishing the bats a good shopping night.
A beaver writes home about building his dam,
While the gulls write rappers: 'I'm not a sham!'

With every note tied with dandelion thread,
Giggles of laughter are joyously spread.
In the world of the woods, let the letters flow,
For in lighthearted laughter, our friendships grow.

Nature's Rustic Ink

With ferns for brushes and mud for ink,
The trees gather 'round for a moment to think.
In nature's classroom, no one's a fool,
Just leaves and twigs making art as a rule.

Beetles provide insights, oh what a scene,
As the daisies giggle and embrace the green.
The sun sets low, casting shadows so neat,
While crickets hum softly, dancing to beat.

With acorns and berries in colors so bright,
Nature's canvas bursts forth with delight.
The flowers compose verses with petals unfurled,
In a gallery vibrant, their secrets are swirled.

So listen and laugh as the wild does its thing,
In rust-colored ink, life's a whimsical fling.
In every small moment, find joy that won't cease,
For nature's a poet, crafting pure peace.

Whispers of the Ancient Wood

In the woods where secrets creep,
A squirrel tells stories, oh so deep.
The trees chuckle with leaves so green,
Where giggles of branches can often be seen.

A wise owl hoots, wearing spectacles snug,
While critters dance round, a merry little bug.
Nature's joke, it tickles the breeze,
Funny how laughter can bounce off the trees.

The Enigma of a Fallen Cone

An acorn asked a pinecone one day,
'Why do you roll and sway in your play?'
The pinecone replied with a chuckling grin,
'Seeking a dance partner, where do I begin?'

It tumbled down hills with flair so bright,
Chasing its dreams on a starry night.
With each little roll, it spread so much cheer,
The forest echoed, 'Come twirl over here!'

Breathing Life into Stillness

In shadows where branches reach for the sun,
A giggling breeze whispers, 'Let's have some fun!'
Mossy carpets spring up for a laugh,
While logs join in a mid-wood craft.

Creatures peek out, with grins on their face,
In the stillness, they frolic, a wild little race.
Every rustle and chime is a comedic sketch,
Nature's own circus, without a single fetch.

Hidden Growth in the Woodlands

Beneath the tall pines, mushrooms conspire,
To tickle your feet with their whimsical choir.
They giggle and jostle in a color parade,
A sprightly display, never to fade.

Decomposing laughter fills the air,
As fungi dance in their fragrant affair.
Each sprout a comedian, unaware of their role,
Creating a stage that swells to its goal.

The Elegance of the Evergreen

In the forest, tall and bright,
Trees wear crowns of green delight.
Squirrels dance, oh what a sight,
Beneath the branches, life feels right.

Boughs and needles, all in jest,
Nature's comedy, we're all guests.
Frolicking critters, they know best,
Amidst the tall, they laugh and rest.

Wind whispers secrets, quite absurd,
A clever chatter of leaf and bird.
Even the worms have thoughts inferred,
In this jolly realm, all is heard.

Dancing shadows, a merry game,
Branches sway, no tree is tame.
In this laughter, we feel the same,
With evergreen grace, none feel shame.

Whispers of the Forest Floor

The ground is rich with giggles and grins,
Where mushrooms pop and play like twins.
Ants march on in their tiny bins,
Nature's laughter always wins.

Leaves rustle softly, shh, don't shout,
Listen close, there's fun about.
Critters skitter, no doubt,
In this party, there's no route.

Rabbits hop, with joy they prance,
Each leap and bound a silly dance.
Every leaf gives chance for chance,
In this woodland, we're all in romance.

With laughter, the forest starts to bloom,
A world where giggles chase the gloom.
In quiet corners, fun finds room,
On the forest floor, joy's in full zoom.

Nature's Spiral Secrets

In spirals of pine, secrets spin,
Who knew nature could wear a grin?
Twisting tales, where all begin,
A whirlwind of joy, oh what a win!

Beneath the bark, jokes intertwine,
With every curl, a punchline shines.
Mice whisper, 'Let's sip some wine,'
In the depths of roots, where laughter climbs.

Tiny acorns plot and scheme,
Their ambitions bigger than they seem.
In their world, they reign supreme,
Chasing each other in a silly dream.

Around each turn, there's fun anew,
Nature's tricks always ensue.
Underneath skies, so bright and blue,
In spirals of secrets, laughter grew.

Guardians of the Woodland

Tall and proud, they stand in line,
Guardians with a sense of rhyme.
Their barks hold stories, oh so fine,
In every creak, a joke's divine.

Fungi peek out with cheeky grins,
Chasing off the silliest sins.
With every twist, the fun begins,
In laughter, the woodland always wins.

They wave to the clouds, as if to say,
'We're the stars in this leafy play!'
Embracing the night, they dance and sway,
In this symphony, the gloom's kept at bay.

So cheer for the trees, the silly crew,
In every rustle, they laugh with you.
Guardians of laughter in shades of hue,
In the woodland's heart, joy's forever true.

The Cones' Legacy

In the forest, cones drop with a thud,
Some bounce like they're in a mud.
Squirrels giggle as they hoard their prize,
While the trees chuckle, under sunny skies.

Old cones gossip of days gone past,
With tales of storms that didn't last.
"Once I was a tree's finest hat!"
Said a cone with a sheen, oh how it sat!

Little kids gather with bags in hand,
Finding treasures all over the land.
But who knew a cone could be so grand?
A nature's trophy, some might have planned.

So next time you stroll by the pines,
Remember the laughter that intertwines.
Join in the fun, let your heart extend,
Together with cones, let the joy not end!

Where the Foxes Roam

On a hill where the foxes love to play,
They leap and dance in a funny ballet.
Pine cones tumble, a raucous race,
As the foxes chase with a comical pace.

Underneath a tree, they find a stash,
Of googly-eyed cones that cause quite a clash.
"What are these gems?" one fox inquires,
"Let's wear them as hats, ignite our desires!"

They mold their pine treasures into fine gear,
With a swirl of laughter, spreading cheer.
Each cone on a head, a crown of delight,
Making all other critters take flight!

So if you roam where these foxes are,
Join their antics, it's sure to go far.
For laughter and cones are the best of friends,
In a merry land where the fun never ends!

Reflecting in Leafy Mirrors

In the glade where the leaves flutter low,
Pine cones gather and put on a show.
They practice their poses in leafy mirrors,
Striking up smiles and giggles of cheerers.

One cone wore a leaf as a bright bow tie,
While others crafted wigs that reached the sky.
"Look at me!" shouted one full of spunk,
As they twirled around like a goofball punk.

Under the sun, they dance and gleam,
With funny tales that spill like a dream.
"I once rolled downhill and caused quite a scene!"
They laugh and they tumble, light and serene.

As dusk fades in, their antics won't cease,
For among the pines, there's joy and peace.
So visit this spot if you crave a grin,
Where the cones and the leaves invite you in!

Fragments of Forgotten Bands

Amidst the trees, a rhythm is found,
A band of cones playing all around.
With sticks as guitars and bark as the beat,
They jam in a circle, oh what a treat!

The drummer's a squirrel, he keeps it on time,
While nearby a rabbit hops, feeling sublime.
The tunes are silly, the lyrics a hoot,
When a hedgehog joins in, it's quite the pursuit!

Old pine cones reminisce their hard days,
Of falling from branches in the wildest plays.
They strum up those memories with laughter and cheer,
As the woodland crowd draws ever so near.

So if you wander to where cones convene,
Join their concert, it's sure to be seen.
For in fun and in music, life's truly grand,
With fragments of joy from this whimsical band!

Cradle of the Earth's Memory

In the forest's embrace, I found a hat,
Made of twigs and leaves, oh how about that!
A squirrel in disbelief, looked my way,
"Fashionable, no? Just for play!"

Boots made of bark, my toes can't breathe,
Yet I strut and dance, with the greatest ease.
The roots tap their feet to my wild song,
The trees cheer me on, can't be wrong!

A dandelion crown upon my head,
The forest critters laugh, but it's all good! Spread.
I prance and twirl, they roll with glee,
Who knew the woods were this carefree?

So hold your laughter, all ye who roam,
Nature's runway, here I call home.
With every step, a comic affair,
In this cradle, we're all debonair!

Wearers of the Forest's Cloak

Glimmering with dew, what a sight to behold,
A squirrel in a cape, if the truth's to be told.
"Up, up and away!" he yells from a tree,
While I giggle and clap, oh, can't you see?

The rabbits wear pajamas, sprightly and bright,
As owls judge in silence, what a whimsical sight!
With mushrooms as shoes and grass as a scarf,
The forest has fashion that's sure to make you laugh.

A hedgehog in goggles rides a big snail,
While ants in their tuxedos are ready to sail.
Each creature's adorned in a quirky display,
Prancing and spinning, on this fine day!

So let's lift our glasses, filled with acorn brew,
To the wearers of cloaks, both silly and true.
In the woods, it's a party, come join our spree,
The fashion show here is as wild as can be!

Starlight in the Pines

Oh, the stars peek down through the needles and leaves,
   A raccoon adjusts his antlers, mischief he weaves.
    "Look up!" he exclaims, with a twinkle of eyes,
     In this nighttime wonder, our giggles arise.

   The owls sing ballads, no notes ever right,
    While fireflies flutter, lending their light.
    A turtle in moonbeams spins tales of old,
  Of adventures in woods, both funny and bold.

The nighttime romances with shadows that dance,
    As crickets are jivers, they take a chance.
    A fox in a vest serenades the big moon,
It's a whimsical concert, the night ends too soon!

   So gather your friends, let laughter ignite,
With starlight as witness, we'll dance through the night.
 In the pines, every giggle takes wing and it flows,
   In this world of pure wonder, anything goes!

The Scrolls of Seasons Past

In autumn's embrace, a leaf slips and falls,
As I trip over laughter, the forest just calls.
"Remember last winter?" said a squirrel with flair,
"We skated on ice, and we didn't care!"

With spring came the blooms, amidst giggles and grins,
Where bees wore top hats and ants played violins.
A summer of sunshine, oh, what a delight,
As the creatures all danced in the warm golden light.

Now the scrolls are unrolling with tales from each time,
Of snowball fights, pranks, and some nutty sublime.
A hedgehog's lost cap, a raccoon's wild quest,
And the laughter we shared, truly one of the best.

So let's toast to the moments, both funny and grand,
In the playful embrace of this whimsical land.
Each season's a chapter, where laughter won't cease,
In the forest of joy, we find our sweet peace!

The Poetry of Green and Brown

In the forest, a comedy show,
With squirrels rehearsing, putting on a glow.
Branches nodding with leafy glee,
While ants gossip, sipping tea.

The trunks play tag, oh what a sight,
As mossy coats get giggles at night.
The breeze joins in with a playful hum,
Nature's laughter is never glum.

A chipmunk juggles acorns with flair,
While butterflies swirl in the warm air.
The grass whispers jokes to the bees,
Tickling ferns with the lightest of tease.

Oh, what joy in this leafy town,
Where everyone wears a greenish crown.
With humor nestled in each sound,
Life's a puzzle where fun is found.

In the Shade of Evergreen Dreams

Underneath a canopy so grand,
Where visions play and shadows stand.
The trees exchange their quirky tales,
While critters chuckle and turn pale.

A bird on a branch, a comedian true,
Sings of mishaps in the morning dew.
The flowers giggle, the grass claps loud,
As nature performs for the joyful crowd.

The sun peeks in, shakes its head,
At the silly antics that dance in bed.
A fox tells secrets, the owls just swoon,
While the playful brook hums a tune.

Dreams swirl high in the green light,
As laughter echoes, pure delight.
In this bower of jest and jesters,
The shade is cool with nature's testers.

Fallen Voices

A leaf whispers secrets down below,
As pine needles giggle and put on a show.
The ground is a stage for stories untold,
With laughter sprouting as wonders unfold.

A twig trips a chipmunk, what a surprise!
As laughter hatches from bright azure skies.
Fallen nuts roll like marbles in play,
While nature's laughter brightens the day.

Mushrooms chuckle beneath the soft rain,
With fungi jokes that never feel vain.
A sleepy old log creaks with a grin,
As the woodland clowns dive right in.

All around, the humor takes flight,
With sprites and shadows dancing in light.
Oh, how the earth giggles and creeps,
In this realm where humor never sleeps.

Beneath the Pine Canopy

Beneath the pines, a circus awaits,
With acrobatic critters who dance with fate.
The owls act wise, but they can't hide,
The chuckles that burst in the moonlit tide.

The raccoons juggle shiny delights,
As fireflies twinkle like tiny sights.
The pines sway gently, tapping their knees,
While the night blooms with cosmic trees.

A wild mouse recites a play in the dark,
With a squirrel's laugh that leaves a mark.
The rustling leaves join in the fun,
In this leafy world where smiles run.

The stars above wink with laughter so bright,
As pine cones roll in merry delight.
In this haven wrapped in green and brown,
Nature's folly wears a joyful crown.

The Stillness of Harvested Fragments

In a basket of joy, they tumble all,
Nature's jester, standing tall.
Some are lumpy, some are round,
Capricious treasures on the ground.

They poke and prod, as if to say,
"Pick me up, I'm here to play!"
With a giggle, they take their flight,
Rolling around in pure delight.

Each little shape, a story to tell,
Falling free from the towering shell.
Wishing on twirls of ridiculous charm,
Hoping to land on a friendly farm.

When autumn whispers, they join the cheer,
Dancing together, they have no fear.
Just fragments of laughter, bright and spry,
As the crisp leaves crunch and the birds fly by.

Secrets in the Forest's Embrace

Whispers echo between the trees,
Squirrels gossip on autumn's breeze.
With each secret, they twist and turn,
Mischief awaits where the leaves brightly burn.

Nutty ninjas with a sly little grin,
Hiding treasures beneath the skin.
Each nut a puzzle, each cone a clue,
In this forest game, who knew?

Fungi giggle, roots interlace,
Every critter wears a friendly face.
The trunks stand tall, keeping still watch,
On nature's antics, they slyly notch.

In this wild realm, all is a jest,
From the mighty oak to the little nest.
As laughter lingers, the forest sings,
The secrets of autumn—oh, the joy it brings!

Whirlwind of Autumn's Gifts

Round and round, the breeze does blow,
Crazy leaves put on a show.
Chasing cones, oh what a sight,
Battle of acorns in the daylight.

Squirrels leap and dive so bold,
Gathering treasures, both warm and cold.
Giggling nuts, with a plump little pout,
Unearth the magic—the fun's about!

Ribbons of orange, gold, and brown,
Nature's confetti raining down.
Then they tumble, just like this rhyme,
With every swirl, it's party time!

In this whirlwind, not a care,
Laughter spins through the crisp, cool air.
Autumn's gifts, a jolly dance,
Join the fun, take a chance!

The Dance of Seasons

When autumn sweeps in, it comes with flair,
Dancing leaves spin without a care.
Nature's prancers, so wild and free,
Join in the rhythm, do you see?

Squirrels shakin' their bushy tails,
Giggling under the shimmery veils.
Twirling cones and nuts alike,
In this party, there's no hike!

As pumpkins roll, a sight so round,
They bounce and laugh upon the ground.
With each season, a playful jest,
In nature's dance, we're truly blessed.

So let's all join this merry song,
Where every creature can't go wrong.
In the harmony of what we find,
The dance of seasons entertains our mind.

The Age of the Evergreen

In the forest, trees did conspire,
Whispering secrets, setting hearts afire.
Squirrels dressed up in tiny caps,
Hiding nuts behind their little naps.

Mossy creatures dance and twirl,
While the sunlight starts to swirl.
Raccoons plotting, what a sight,
Trying to steal a bird's delight.

Bark and branches laugh in glee,
As the wind hums a silly spree.
Pine needles giggle, falling down,
Dressing the earth in a greenish crown.

Evergreen guards of the wood,
Sharing laughter, feeling good.
In this realm where jokes unwind,
Nature's humor, perfectly blind.

Roots Beneath

Underneath the ground they squirm,
Roots complain, a gnarled term.
Whispering tales, in tangled cues,
Of stolen socks and wandering shoes.

The earthworms laugh, cracking jokes,
While ants march like tiny folks.
Raccoons argue, who's got the stash?
Pointy stones, they dance and clash.

Beneath the bark, the fungi play,
A family reunion, every day.
Little secrets in the dirt,
Spreading laughter with a flirt.

Roots lend support; they are the jest,
A hidden comedy, never at rest.
Grounded jokes, quite absurd,
Best kept quiet, never heard.

Dreams Above

In the canopy, the branches sway,
Birds are gossiping about their day.
Feathers ruffled in comical flare,
While squirrels steal the show with flair.

Clouds drift by, wearing silly hats,
Nomadic wanderers, like fluffy mats.
Dancing shadows of flying dreams,
Chasing giggles and quirky schemes.

Rain drops join the festive beat,
Bouncing off leaves, what a treat!
Nature's jester, sky on the move,
Twisted humor in every groove.

Wild and free, the skies explode,
In a colorful comic ode.
Up above, its laughter reigns,
In the heights where joy remains.

Wanderer Among the Pines

A wanderer lost, with map in hand,
Chasing squirrels, thinking it's grand.
With every turn, they look for signs,
Direction lost, they laugh with pines.

Branches wave, "Join in our fun!"
A game of chase, no end, no run.
The sun peeks through, a playful tease,
Tickling the wanderer with ease.

Logs become couches, so quite posh,
A nap with a woodpecker's josh.
Lost in laughter, they miss their ride,
But joy in pines can't be denied.

What fun it is to roam and roam,
With nature's humor as their home.
A wanderer forever to be,
Chasing joy among the trees.

A Chronicle of Shadows

Shadows dance on the forest floor,
Telling jokes from times of yore.
Figures flicker, making merry,
As if the light had lost its dairy.

Tree trunks shiver with delight,
Sharing tales of the last moonlight.
Bizarre silhouettes think they can sing,
Harmonizing under the pine's ring.

In one corner, a shadow sneezes,
Causing a laugh as it pleases.
Whispered secrets, giggles mix,
A forest full of funny tricks.

Chronicles written in leafy ink,
Where spirits laugh and dancers wink.
In the shadows, all is bright,
A weird, whimsical forest night.

Echoes in the Canopy

Squirrels chatter, they plot and scheme,
While breezes whisper, like a dream.
Acorns tumble with a playful thud,
Nature's chuckle in a leafy bud.

Branches sway with a jolly creak,
The forest giggles, so to speak.
Sunlight dances, a golden glow,
Tickling the trunks with a wink and flow.

Fungi grinning upon the ground,
Mushrooms giggle without a sound.
Beetles boogie, going to town,
In this wild, funny leafy crown.

Laughter echoes in the tall, green trees,
Spreading joy on the gentle breeze.
A pinecone rolls, slips on a pine,
Nature chuckles, "Oh, that's just fine!"

The Silent Seed

A seed sat quietly, tucked in the earth,
Wondering, pondering its future and worth.
It dreamed of sunshine, of growing tall,
   Yet first it giggled—'What if I fall?'

The other seeds whispered, 'Just be brave!'
   'But what if a bird is here to save?'
They snickered softly beneath the ground,
Imagining the mischief that could be found.

Rain came dancing, pattering cheer,
And the seed chuckled, 'At last, I hear!
It's time to sprout with a tiny shout,
I'll pop on up, throw my doubts out.'

Up sprang the seed with a swirl and a twirl,
   Brushing the dirt with a leafy curl.
It waved to the clouds and winked at the sun,
And chuckled, 'Being a tree could be fun!'

Cones and Dreams

A cone on a branch dreams of flight,
It wiggles and jiggly, oh what a sight!
It hopes for a squirrel to give it a toss,
'I'll roll down the hill, yeah, I'll be the boss!'

The pine bough scoffs with a rustling laugh,
'You're stuck here with me, oh little half.
You dream of the wind, but you're glued to this tree,
Just embrace the fun and be silly like me!'

Then a gust rushed by, what a wild ride,
The cone took off, with nowhere to hide.
It spun and it twirled, oh what a parade,
Laughter erupted as it danced unafraid.

On the ground it landed, a bit of a flop,
Yet joyful and proud, it couldn't quite stop.
So cones gather round, in a funny, sweet team,
To share all the giggles from their wild dream.

Dance of the Conifer Leaves

Leaves sway and sway in a merry jig,
A pine needle concert, oh so big.
With every gust, they twist and dive,
A leafy ballet, so alive!

Bugs in tuxedos, all dressed to impress,
Twirling and darting, what a cute mess.
A snail in a top hat, very in style,
Glides past the giggles, making us smile.

The branches clap hands, a whimsical cheer,
As nature's rhythm fills every ear.
The forest floor chuckles, joining the song,
"Keep on dancing, you can't go wrong!"

What a scene of mirth among the trees,
Gusts of laughter float in the breeze.
Each leaf a dancer, so carefree and spry,
In this fun-filled, conifer sky!

The Heart of a Spruce

In a forest where trees stand tall,
The spruce has feelings, can you hear their call?
With branches waving, they dance and sway,
Whispers of wind, come join the play!

A squirrel leaps with a nut to munch,
While the spruce giggles, it's quite the hunch!
With cones like hats upon their heads,
They throw a party among the spreads!

But when the storm makes the branches bend,
The spruce just laughs at the gusty trend.
"I'm strong! I'm tall! I'm filled with glee!"
While everyone else runs under the tree!

So next time you're there, don't hesitate,
Give a spruce a hug, it's never too late!
For the heart of a spruce is full of cheer,
Come share the laughter, it's always near!

Beneath the Veil of Pine Needles

Beneath the needles, what secrets lie?
A gathering of critters, oh me, oh my!
Chipmunks in shadows, they dance and prance,
A game of hide and seek, oh what a chance!

The pine needles laugh, they tickle the toes,
As squirrels spin tales of their climbing woes.
With every rustle, there's a chuckle or two,
Mysteries wrapped in green — who knew?

Fallen cones clutter the forest floor,
Each one a treasure, who could ask for more?
As the raccoons plot and gather with glee,
Their secret stash, a feast for thee!

In the shade of the pines, let's chase the sun,
Beneath the veil, we all can have fun!
So if you hear laughter, don't be surprised,
It's nature's own giggle, only disguised!

Mysterious Gifts of the Conifer

In the land of green, where the conifers grow,
Mysterious gifts, they bestow like a show.
A pinecone falls with a plop and a thud,
It rolls and it tumbles, landing in mud!

What's inside, oh what could it be?
A treasure of seeds? Or a dance party spree?
Nature's own riddle, you scratch your head,
While squirrels plot mischief, in the branches, they tread!

Gifts from above, falling without pause,
Wreathed in pine scent, deserving of applause.
The forest holds secrets behind every bough,
Just nibble a cone and see how it's wowed!

So traipse through the pines, with joy in your heart,
The gifts of the conifer are just the start.
With humor and warmth, they invite us to play,
Join in the fun, let's laugh all day!

Nature's Artistry Unfurled

Oh look at the trees, they wear quite the garb,
With cones like jewels in a grand green arb.
Their branches create a whimsical dance,
As the wind gives a giggle, they leap at the chance!

Artistry painted in hues of green,
Each needle and twig, a sight to be seen.
The forest's a canvas, wild and free,
With brush strokes of laughter, come join in glee!

Pinecones like sculptures, each one a delight,
They scatter the ground, a fanciful sight.
With every cone drop, the trees throw a feast,
Crafting nature's laugh, in the forest's beast!

So traipse through the arts, let your spirit fly,
Nature's own gallery under the sky.
For humor and beauty are woven in twine,
In this grand masterpiece, let your heart shine!

A Symphony in Cones

Upon the branch, a cone does dance,
Shaking its scales, to chance a glance.
It twirls and spins, with quite a flair,
As squirrels giggle, without a care.

The wind begins to play its tune,
The cones clap back, a wild festoon.
With every rustle, a laugh takes flight,
Nature's concert, pure delight!

Behold the cone, a nature's jest,
A little prankster, never at rest.
It invents a game, who can catch?
The acorn drops, what a mismatched!

Adorned with seeds, like tiny hats,
It boasts and brags among the brats.
A king of jest in the forest wide,
With laughter echoing, side by side.

Rustling Secrets

Amidst tall pines, secrets are spun,
Whispers of squirrels, all in fun.
The cones conspire, oh what a crowd,
With giggles and grins, they're feeling proud.

Rustling leaves, a playful sound,
In the underbrush, laughs abound.
A cone drops down, 'I've had enough!'
With a thud, it sighs, 'This game is rough!'

The shadows flicker, as jokes fly high,
In the forest, where time passes by.
The cones, they chuckle at every scene,
Juggling laughter beneath the green.

Under moonlit skies, they revel and cheer,
Playing tag, from far and near.
Each tumble, a story, a giggle to share,
Rustling secrets, floating in the air.

Musings from Pine Shadows

In the shade of pines, we find our muse,
Where cones put on their best shoes.
Do they roller-skate or take a ride?
No one knows, they're full of pride!

With each soft rustle, they share a laugh,
Pondering jokes from nature's staff.
What's a tree's favorite dance? Oh, how fun!
The branch jiggle, when faced with the sun!

Silly seeds, in fanciful dreams,
Bouncing around like playful beams.
As they tumble down, they shout with glee,
'Catch me if you can, oh just you see!'

In these shadows, mischief blooms,
With giggles echoing through darkened rooms.
So here we sit, beneath pine crowns,
Chortling together, brushing off frowns.

Life in the Underbrush

In the underbrush, life's a delight,
Where cones are jesters, bursting with light.
They tumble down, creating a riot,
With furry friends, oh what a diet!

A chipmunk scurries, with speed and grace,
Chasing the cones in a wild race.
With every thud, a story begins,
Of playful mischief and furry grins.

There's laughter buried in leaves so deep,
Where secrets in cones are hidden to keep.
What do they say when the sun's in sight?
'Let's have a party, under moonlight!'

So let us gather, in this forest round,
And share all the fun that is waiting to be found.
For in the underbrush, with cones all around,
The funniest tales of life abound!

Vestiges of Ancient Growth

In a forest where squirrels conspire,
Old trees hold tales, never tire.
Their roots gossip beneath the dirt,
While mushrooms wear hats, looking quite flirt.

With every step, a crunching sound,
Yearning for treasures to be found.
Beneath the branches, shadows dance,
I trip over roots, miss my chance!

The wise old oaks, with beards of moss,
Chuckle softly at my loss.
A deer bursts forth, a jealous prank,
While I'm stuck on a poor pine plank.

Laughter echoes through the trees,
As leaves flutter down with such ease.
I grab a handful, tickled pink,
And dash away, quick as a wink.

Treetops' Gallery

In the treetops, a gallery thrives,
With wobbly branches, each truly jives.
Painted with hues of green and brown,
It's nature's circus; no need for a crown.

A squirrel barista serves acorn lattes,
While chipmunks debate, with wild strategies.
Parrots gossip about misfit seeds,
While the clumsy woodpecker takes lead.

Artists in the branches paint with flair,
Each nut and leaf a masterpiece rare.
With boisterous giggles as their guide,
They create the art of the wild side.

So next time you ponder a stroll,
Look above, let nature console.
The treetops' gallery, wild and free,
Is filled with fun, just come see!

Ethereal Pine Duets

Two pines stand tall, a duet they sing,
Rustling needles, a whimsical thing.
With a twist and a turn, they sway to the beat,
As squirrels join in for a tree-top feat.

Each note is a whisper of wind's delight,
A dance of the branches, a comical sight.
With acorn maracas, they shake and they groove,
While rabbits tap dance in a joyful move.

The boughs wave like arms in a jubilant show,
As the sun shines down with a golden glow.
Beneath this circus of needles and cheer,
I can't help but laugh, it's that time of year.

Oh, ethereal pines, keep the humor alive,
In the forest carnival where creatures connive.
Each day is a tune, each night, a delight,
In the world of the pines, everything feels right.

Whispers in the Wind

Whispers float gently through the pines,
Chirps of the birds mixed with clever lines.
A breeze stirs up gossip, oh what a plot,
As chipmunks debate, who forgot the nut pot?

Beneath the branches, shadows unfold,
The laughter of rabbits, timid but bold.
Each rustling leaf, a playful tease,
As nature spins tales in the summer breeze.

A squirrel scampers, a thief in the trees,
Stealing my snack with the greatest of ease.
"Hey, come back here!" I shout with a grin,
But he's too busy, he's bound to win.

So listen closely to the wind's playful dance,
In the realm of the pines, there's always a chance.
To giggle with nature, to chuckle and grin,
Embrace all the whispers, let the joy begin!

Whispers from the Forest Floor

In the woods, the squirrels chat,
They giggle as they chase a cat.
Leaves rustle with a secret tale,
Even mushrooms sport a grin, won't fail.

A pine needle's tickle makes me sneeze,
The branches wave; oh, such a tease!
Beneath the boughs, a frog does croak,
"Who knew a stick could wear a cloak?"

Acorns fall with a goofy thud,
Nature's laughter turns to mud.
The rabbits bounce with merry glee,
It's a wild party, come and see!

So next time you stroll through the trees,
Listen close for the forest's glee.
With every step, let your heart soar,
Join in the whispers from the forest floor!

The Dance of Nature's Secrets

In the glade, the critters sway,
The bushes giggle in a playful way.
Moss carpets soft, a bouncy stage,
For rabbits waltzing, setting the age.

A beetle twirls, not shy at all,
While a squirrel hiccups, takes a fall.
The pines are clapping, their cones in tow,
What a sight, this nature's show!

Underneath the ferns, a party's in play,
The shadows snap, they're here to stay.
With whispers of secrets, the trees confide,
"Join our dance, let's rule the wild side!"

In laughter and joy, the forest spins,
With nature's groove, everyone wins.
Next time you walk through the green retreat,
Remember, nature's dance can be quite the treat!

Echoes of Evergreen Dreams

In the twilight, the pines hum sweet,
Whispers of dreams dance on our feet.
A raccoon's snicker, the moonlit gleam,
Nature giggles, life's a dream.

Acorns roll like tiny balls,
Down the hill, they bounce and fall.
The owls' winks, a sly surprise,
In the forest's joy, the mischief lies.

A chipmunk jives with a joyful squeak,
While loons croon in harmony's peak.
The echoes of laughter ring out clear,
Join the fun, come lend an ear!

So under the stars, let your heart beam,
With giggles woven in nature's seam.
In the whispers of night, find your theme,
For together we laugh in evergreen dreams!

Secrets in the Silence of Pines

Silence falls, yet giggles creep,
In the quiet, the forest keeps.
A twig snaps like an old man's joke,
Watch for laughter, don't miss the poke!

The pines hold secrets, it's vast and grand,
With whispers traded by the land.
A crunch of leaves, a chuckle found,
In the stillness, joy is bound.

A fox slips through with a playful grin,
A game of tag about to begin.
With rustling coats, they spin and twirl,
Each leap draws out a joyous swirl.

So step lightly on this earthy stage,
Unlock the forest's light-hearted page.
Among the tall trees, let your worries decline,
Find the laughter in the secrets of pines!

Whiskers of the Wild

In the forest, a whisker stepped,
Wobbly and wild, it boldly swept.
Tails in the air, they danced a jig,
A furry parade, oh what a gig!

Squirrels in hats, looking quite grand,
Tiptoeing through with a bowl of sand.
The raccoon chef flips pancakes high,
But misses a catch – oh my, oh my!

Frogs croak the beat, they're very wise,
While pondering snacks and giant fries.
Every whisker, a story to tell,
In the wild they laugh, all is swell!

So come take a stroll, don't be so shy,
Join the antics where creatures fly.
The wittiest whiskers, full of cheer,
In the forest of fun, let's all steer!

Balancing on the Brink

A squirrel named Chip, with skills divine,
Tried tightrope walking on a thin line.
With acorns in hand and a cheeky grin,
He danced on the brink – let the fun begin!

The birds cheered loudly from their high trees,
"Look at him go! What a sight to see!"
But whoops! slipped a paw, and down he did fall,
He landed right in a deep, leafy squall!

The critters all laughed, 'twas quite the show,
While Chip peeked out with a squeaky "Hello!"
He climbed back up, with a brand new plan,
To juggle his nuts like a true circus man!

So life on the brink's quite a thrill,
With twirling and laughter, we all can chill.
Next time you slip, don't let it sting,
Embrace the joy of balancing!

Forest Feathers

Fluffy old owls in colorful hats,
Wobbled and giggled, laughing like brats.
Chickens with wings, who knew how to sing,
They strut in the woods like a feathered king!

A parrot named Pete, with jokes galore,
Cracked up the woods, we begged him for more.
"Why did the bird go to the mall?"
"To buy some new chirps and a feather ball!"

The crows in the branches rolled over in glee,
Their cawing was loud, like a wild spree.
"Let's throw a party, it's feather day!"
And off they all flew, in a bright ballet!

So down in the woods with friends oh so neat,
Feathers and laughter make life so sweet.
Join in the fun, let your spirit soar,
In this feathered fest, there's always more!

Guardians of the Glade

The guardians gather at nightfall's light,
With giggles and whispers, what a delight!
Bats on a mission, with capes on their backs,
Fly through the trees, avoiding the cracks!

The hedgehogs hold court, with tales to share,
Of nighttime adventures beyond all compare.
"Did you see that thing with the big floppy ears?"
"What? A creature that ticks? Oh, give me some cheers!"

With huddles of chuckles, the owls swoop by,
Trading sweet secrets, while stars twinkle high.
"Safety in numbers, let's guard the night!"
Patrol of the glade, what a comical sight!

So if you hear laughter where shadows blend,
Know it's the guardians, your very best friends.
In the heart of the night, their giggles unite,
Protecting the glade with joy and delight!

When Needles Fall in Time

When needles drop from towering pine,
They start a party, oh so divine.
Squirrels dance with a joyful face,
While owls groove at their own pace.

The forest floor becomes their stage,
As laughter bursts like a well-worn page.
Each needle twirls in the autumn breeze,
While mice join in with a jig and tease.

A deer peeks in with a curious glance,
Wondering if she too can dance.
The trees all sway, a lively crew,
With nature's rhythm, they'll break right through.

In this wild, woodsy cabaret,
Where prickly needles lead the way,
Just sit back, relax, and unwind,
As nature's humor plays, one of a kind.

A Tapestry of Woodland Tales

In the forest, stories bloom,
As branches chuckle, dispelling gloom.
A squirrel's mishap with an acorn round,
Sends giggles echoing all around.

The fox, with flair, spins grand illusions,
Crafting dramas with crafty conclusions.
He claims a tail with sparkling hue,
While rabbits sneak a peek at the view.

A tale of a chipmunk's bountiful stash,
Of cheese and nuts, he'd fiercely bash.
Each woodland critter whispers in cheer,
As they sip on laughter, loud and clear.

This tapestry of giggles we weave,
With every whisper and playful pleat.
So gather round, let the tales unfold,
In wondrous woods, where fun is bold.

The Cones That Collect the Rain

The cones above sway, a comical sight,
As they huddle close, preparing for flight.
They catch raindrops, oh what a spree,
Turning drizzles into a jubilee.

Droplets tumble, a slippery race,
As pine cones giggle in the wet embrace.
A party ensues with splashes and splatter,
Bringing joy to the woodland chatter.

With every drip, they bounce and spin,
Chasing puddles, they leap right in.
The forest erupts in a fit of cheer,
For these little heroes, we hold so dear.

So next time it rains, don't forget to glance,
At those playful cones, leading the dance.
In nature's circus, where fun takes flight,
The cones are the stars, shining so bright.

Beneath the Boughs of Time

Beneath the boughs, the laughter flows,
Where every creature strikes a pose.
A raccoon brags of his shiny loot,
While the possum plays a flute-like hoot.

Time stands still in this playful nook,
As secrets rustle like a storybook.
Chipmunks swap tales, bold and spry,
While shadows giggle as they flit by.

The wise old owl, with a wink so sly,
Watches below with a twinkling eye.
As laughter dances through leaves so green,
In this woodland wonder, the fun's routine.

With each tick of time, more jesters appear,
Crafting tales filled with humor and cheer.
Beneath the boughs where the stories rhyme,
We celebrate life… such a hilarious time!

Footprints in Nature's Diary

In the forest, I left a trace,
A muddy shoe and a squirrel's face.
Nature chuckled, the leaves did sway,
As I slipped and tumbled away.

Birds cawed loud, I looked like a clown,
Tripping over roots that pulled me down.
The path, it giggled, with every bounce,
As I tried to act like I wasn't a flounce.

The trees were wise, they'd seen it all,
A dance of fail, in the pine-tree hall.
I waved to them, they shook their limbs,
Saying, "Come join us, in our silly whims!"

Nature's diary, it fills with cheer,
Footprints and laughs, from far and near.
So if you wander on this trail so wide,
Bring your giggles, and take the ride!

Ephemeral Echoes

Whispers of laughter, carried on air,
Echoes that dance without a care.
Like pine needles falling, soft and light,
They tickle the ground, just out of sight.

A friendly gust gives a playful shove,
Pine cones tumble, oh what a love!
One hit my head, I burst into giggles,
The forest erupted, with shaking wiggles.

In shadows, a creature peeks with glee,
"Who's this fool, befalling on me?"
I wink at the squirrel, he winks right back,
In this symphony of nature, we lose track.

A fleeting moment, just a quick laugh,
Nature's humor, a whimsical path.
So listen closely to each pine-sweet sound,
Ephemeral echoes where joy is found!

Tranquil Pines and the Human Heart

In tranquil pines, I found my beat,
Heartstrings strumming, oh how sweet!
But a branch above dropped like a lead,
I shuffled in embarrassment instead.

A heart so calm, now racing wild,
Nature's melody, oh how it smiled!
The breeze played tricks, tickling my ears,
As laughter erupted, chasing my fears.

Each pine stood tall, like a wise old sage,
Reading my heart like an open page.
At times it felt like a comic show,
With faces of bark, an audience to blow.

Yet in that moment, all worries took flight,
Tranquil pines shed burdens light.
With laughter and roots intertwining tight,
My heart danced free, in nature's delight!

Memories Scattered Below

Memories scattered beneath the trees,
Like acorns dropped by teasing breeze.
I tripped on a thought, fell into a smile,
Nature's own circus, with style and guile.

Each step a giggle, each glance a jest,
Pine needles whispering their quirky quest.
Old logs laid out, like stories told,
Of woodland mischief, young and old.

The forest floor, a tapestry grand,
With feel-good flukes, and truths unplanned.
I laughed at a shadow that danced in the light,
A game of pretend till the day turned bright.

So gather your stories, let laughter unwind,
In nature's embrace, we're never maligned.
With echoes of joy, together we roam,
In this splendid forest, we find our home!

www.ingramcontent.com/pod-product-compliance
Lightning Source LLC
Chambersburg PA
CBHW071829160426
43209CB00003B/246